BEFORE YOU BEGIN...

Make sure to download the FREE audio program for this book which comes with your purchase! Just go to

www.slangman.com/audio

then look for your book and enter this code:

E2G3EZC1N7LY

Beauty and the Beast

Written by: David Burke
Copy Editor: Julie Bobrick
Illustrated by: "Migs!" Sandoval
Translator: Deese & Petra Wirth
Proofreader: Kai Cofer

Copyright © 2017 by David Burke

Email: info@heywordy.com
Website: www.heywordy.com

Hey Wordy! and all related characters and elements are © and trademarks of Hey Wordy, LLC.

Published by Slangman Publishing. Slangman is a registered trademark of David Burke. All rights reserved. Reproduction or translation of any part of this work beyond that permitted by section 107 or 108 of the 1976 United States Copyright Act without the permission of the copyright owner is unlawful. Requests for permission or further information should be addressed to the Permissions Department, Slangman Publishing. This publication is designed to provide accurate and authoritative information in regard to the subject matter covered. The persons, entities and events in this book are fictitious. Any similarities with actual persons or entities, past and present, are purely coincidental.

ISBN13: 978-1-891888-46-5

Printed in the U.S.A.

Meet the Author
David Burke

Creator and star of the children's TV show, *Hey Wordy!*, David Burke has been single-handedly revolutionizing the foreign language-learning movement worldwide.

In addition to being a performer of boundless energy and enthusiasm, David speaks seven languages. A successful author and entrepreneur, he has built a thriving international publishing company featuring over 100 books he has written for teen/adults & children. His books have won publishing awards and have sold more than one million copies. David's Street Speak™ and Biz Speak™ series of books and audio programs are used around the world by government agencies, leading universities and major corporations.

Since age 4, David has been a classically trained pianist and uses his musical gifts to compose and perform original songs for his TV series, *Hey Wordy!* which introduces children to foreign languages and cultures through music, animation, and magical adventures. He has also composed, orchestrated, and performed all the music in the audio programs for each of these books.

David's engaging and charismatic persona became a fixture on broadcast entertainment channels around the world, such as CNN and the BBC. David and his work have been highlighted in many major publications, including The Los Angeles Times, The Chicago Tribune and The Christian Science Monitor.

"This series teaches everyday words that occur in your child's life, as well as terms having to do with politeness, greetings, family & friendship."

David Burke

German vocabulary taught:

Bestie = beast
bitte = please
fünf = five
Garten = garden
Geschenk = gift
guten Tag = hello
Halskette = necklace
häßlich = ugly
Herr = sir
ich liebe dich = I love you
Mittag = noon
Mittagessen = lunch
nett = kind
Pferd = horse
Reise = trip
Ring = ring
Rose = rose
sechs = six
sehr = very much
Tochter = daughter
vier = four

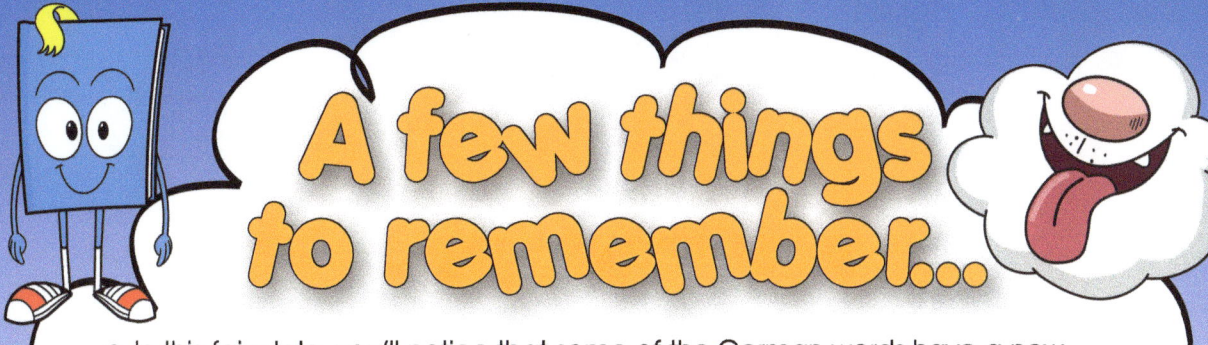

A few things to remember...

- In this fairy tale, you'll notice that some of the German words have a new letter of the alphabet. It's the letter "ß" which looks a lot like our letter "B," but it's not! It's called an "eszett" which is used to represent "ss." For example:

    foot = **Fuss**, but it's always written as **Fuß**.
    big = **gross**, but it's always written as **groß**.

- You'll notice that in German, all nouns (those words that represent a person, place, or thing) begin with an uppercase letter. That's because in German, ALL nouns are written this way! For example:

    girl=**Mädchen** • house=**Haus** • party=**Fest** • prince=**Prinz**

from Cindellera (Level 1)

auf Wiedersehen = goodbye
böse = mean
danke = thank you
Fest = party
Frau = wife
Fuß = foot
gern geschehen = you're welcome
glücklich = happy
groß = big
Haus = house

hübsch = pretty
Kleid = dress
Mädchen = girl
Moment = moment
Mitternacht = midnight
Prinz = prince
Schuh = shoe
stattlich = handsome
traurig = sad
verliebt = in love

from Goldilocks & The Three Bears (Level 2)

Babybär = baby bear
Bär = bear
Bett = bed
drei = three
eins = one
hart = hard
heiß = hot
kalt = cold
klein = little
Küche = kitchen

Mama = mama
müde = tired
Papa = papa
Schüssel = bowl
Sessel = armchair
Spaziergang = stroll
Tisch = table
Tür = door
weich = soft
zwei = two

Tochter

sehr

Once upon a time, there was a *Papa* who had an eldest daughter, Julie, a middle **Tochter**, Tessa, and a youngest **Tochter** named Belle. He loved them very much. He was getting ready to take a long [trip] and asked each **Tochter**, "What can I bring you from my **Reise**?" "I'd like a [ring] to wear on my finger," said Julie. "I'd like a [necklace] to wear around my neck." said Tessa.

3

But Belle, who was the most *hübsch* of all said, "Please. I don't want a **Ring** to wear on my finger or a **Halskette** to wear around my neck. All I want is a rose." He replied, "You shall

Bitte → Please
Rose → rose

each receive your gift." "Oh, *danke* **sehr**!" said each **Tochter**. Then their *Papa* mounted his horse and they shouted, "Have a good **Reise**, *Papa*! We will miss you **sehr**!"

Geschenk

Pferd

As he rode off, each **Tochter** shouted again, "*Auf Wiedersehen, Papa! Auf Wiedersehen!*" until he was out of sight. When it was time for him to return, he first stopped to buy a **Ring** for his eldest

Tochter to wear on her finger, a **Halskette** for his second **Tochter** to wear around her neck, but he waited to get closer to his *Haus* to look for a garden where he could find a **Rose** for

Garten

Belle. After a few hours, he saw a magnificent **Garten**. He got off his **Pferd**, walked into the **Garten** and picked a **Rose** that was the most *hübsch* he'd ever seen. At that very **Moment**, the *Tür* to the *Haus* opened and a beast who was very *groß* came out and ran toward him. "Who stole a **Rose** from my **Garten**?" exploded the **Bestie**. "*Bitte*, Sir !" said the *Papa*.

Bestie

Herr

"**Bitte**, don't hurt me, **Herr**. I promised my **Tochter** that I'd bring her a **Rose** as a **Geschenk** after my long **Reise**. It was just ONE **Rose** from your **Garten**!" "It's still stealing!" said the **Bestie**. "I will spare your life if you bring me the **Tochter** you speak of by noon in six days. Here she will live the rest of her life." Naturally, the

Mittag

sechs

Papa was very *traurig* by this request, but he promised to return with Belle at **Mittag** in **sechs** days. As he arrived at his *Haus*, each **Tochter** rushed out to greet him. He gave them each the **Geschenk** they'd asked for. Each **Tochter** was very *glücklich* and shouted, "*Danke* **sehr**, Papa!" "*Gern geschehen!*" he replied. But he was still *traurig* because he had to tell Belle

13

ich liebe dich

about the promise he'd made with the **Bestie**. "Belle, I love you. **Ich liebe dich sehr** and want you to be *glücklich*. But I must tell you what I have done..." Her *Papa* went on to explain what had happened that day and about the promise he had made. He warned her about how [ugly] the **Bestie** was, but Belle felt responsible because the **Rose** was a **Geschenk**

→ **häßlich**

she'd requested. So she agreed to go. **Sechs** days passed quickly and it was time to leave. Her sisters were very *traurig* to say *auf Wiedersehen* to Belle but they understood that she had no choice.

So Belle and her *Papa* mounted the **Pferd** and rode off. They arrived at exactly **Mittag** as instructed. Belle and her *Papa* got off the **Pferd** and approached the *Haus* of the **Bestie**.

Guten Tag

The *Tür* opened slowly and they walked in. "Hello!" said the *Papa*. "**Guten Tag**!" But there was no answer. As they walked in, they saw a *Tisch* in the middle of the *Küche* filled with food.

It looked like someone was having a *Fest*! Just then they heard a deep voice say, "**Guten Tag**. This [lunch] is especially for you. **Bitte**, enjoy!" Not wanting to be impolite, they began eating

Mittagessen

the magnificent **Mittagessen** before them. And so many desserts! Belle was so excited and already busily counting them. "...four, five, **sechs**. **Sechs** different, wonderful desserts!

vier
fünf

She counted them again just to make sure, "**Eins**, **zwei**, **drei**, **vier**, **fünf**, **sechs**! It was true! **Sechs** delicious desserts all for them! They had never seen a more wonderful

Mittagessen in their lives! Suddenly, they heard footsteps approaching. There he was – the **Bestie** himself. Indeed, he was truly **häßlich**. Scared, Belle said, "**Guten Tag**,

Herr and *danke* **sehr** for the delicious **Mittagessen**." "*Gern geschehen*," replied the **Bestie**. He seemed very kind toward Belle. → **nett**
Her *Papa* was permitted to come visit her every

week which made her very *glücklich*. He gave Belle a kiss on the cheek, mounted his **Pferd**, and said, "*Auf Wiedersehen*, Belle. **Ich liebe dich sehr**, my **Tochter**!" and rode off back to his

Haus. At that **Moment**, the **Bestie** turned toward Belle and said, "**Bitte**. What's mine is yours. I will return every day at **Mittag** to see you." He then quickly ran off, leaving Belle alone.

Because he was so **nett** toward her, Belle was no longer afraid, and was even *glücklich* when he came to visit at **Mittag**. Every day, they laughed more and more and enjoyed sharing stories with each other. But one day, the **Bestie** didn't arrive at **Mittag** as usual. So, Belle went to look for him. She walked outside into the

Garten and there he was lying on the ground lifeless. Belle cried, "Oh, why did you have to die? **Ich liebe dich**! **Ich liebe dich sehr**!" She gave him a kiss on the cheek and suddenly, right before her eyes, he awoke and was transformed into a *Prinz* who was very *stattlich*, indeed! He explained to her that a *böse* magician had changed him into a **Bestie** and only the kiss of a **Mädchen** who was *verliebt* with him, and the words "**Ich liebe dich**," could change him back. The next day at **Mittag**, Belle became his *Frau*, and they all lived happily ever after.

Now you're ready for Levels 4 & 5!

Levels 4 & 5 contain the words from Levels 1, 2 and 3 plus all NEW words!

For more HEY WORDY! products, visit...

www.ingramcontent.com/pod-product-compliance
Lightning Source LLC
Chambersburg PA
CBHW042030100526
44587CB00029B/4364